# The Runner of Little Races

## by

## Ray Diamond

# The Runner of Little Races

ISBN – 13: 978-1-906374-01-3

A CIP record for this title is available from the British Library.

Published by Black Box Publications.

Printed in the UK by CPI Bookmarque, Croydon, CR0 4TD

The painting on the front cover is *Tondal's Vision* by a follower of Hieronymus Bosch.

# **CONTENTS**

## **PROLOGUE**

## **ON THE PAST**

## **ON BEAUTY**

## **SELF - PORTRAIT**

## THE PRESENT

## TERROR

## HAVE YOUR SAY

## THE LITERARY SCENE

## THE FUTURE

## ON THE SOUL

**PROLOGUE →**

# A BALANCED POEM

In this poem I have achieved a balance
Between male and female characters

Thank goodness I don't write in French!
*La table* balanced by *le garcon*, etc.

The author is homosexual,
The main protagonist, lesbian,
And although there is
Only one person in a wheelchair,
There *are* three references to the Holocaust

I tread the proper line between scepticism
And outright denial, of course,
And God is present only in his absence

The punctuation is democratic
I.e. to be filled in by the reader

I have eschewed complex and unusual vocabulary

(*Cut the word "eschew"*)

I know *I* am writing the poem
And you are only the reader,
But, as in quantum physics,
The observer
Is an integral part of the whole process

Besides, I hereby promise to read any one poem
Of similar length and content
That any of you may produce in the future

(*Excise the reference to quantum physics*)

(*Excise the word "excise"*)

The work has been spell-checked,
Is guaranteed free of defamatory subject matter,
And has a certificate of hygiene
Covering all viruses, excluding bird-flu.

I offer it to you without let or hindrance,
On the understanding that any views expressed
Are purely my own, and without wider significance.

I write in the English tradition,
While recognising the worth and importance
Of all other literary traditions,
Excluding those now deemed officially unworthy

I hope you enjoy it!

But I can accept no responsibility
For personal loss or injury occasioned
By its perusal.

**WARNING: THIS PRODUCT MAY CONTAIN
TRACES OF IRONY.**

Thank you.

# ON THE PAST →

# VIRTUAL MOTHER

My mother isn't human enough to get ill
She just rubs away like a stone
With the action of time,
Or stiffens up slightly, and goes grey
Like an old dog

Her imagination doesn't stretch as far as cancer
Or heart-disease
Though she's taken to dementia
Like a duck to water

She's not adrift in modernity
Like some old people –
The T.V. manifested itself in her living room
With all the familiarity of an extraterrestrial
Popped in to borrow
A coronation mug of sugar

She still shouts down the telephone
When phoning long-distance

But issues driving instructions confidently enough
From any back seat
Fully conversant, it appears,
With automatic gear-change,
And satellite navigation

She detects a certain shift in skin colour
At the local post office,
But female vicars, and gay marriages
Are still below the radar

She swims like a somnambulist
Through a sea of microwaves
Will happily bounce virtual particles
Off indeterminate screens,
If, as a result,
She can eat a TV snack
And watch EastEnders

My mother is too much a creature of habit
To do anything as novel as dying

But she might flick channels

'Til she finds a blank one

# WHERE ARE THEY NOW?

I've had several lives,
But this one is the worst –

Now my knees are bent
From delivering leaflets –
Cross-examining the radio,
Applying pressure,

Where are they now?

Joan Baez killing babies in Mongolia;
Jimmy Tarbuck condemned to solitary confinement
Inside himself;
Dan Quayle denying the Holocaust
In some African village.

Where are any of us now?
Having had our five minutes of fame,
At the unplugged mike
In the open sewer

Making brash statements about the weather,
Causing controversy

How many artists have *you* fucked?
Excluding yourself...

# I DIED AS A CHILD

I'm not certain I didn't die as a child

The signs are all there

Run over by a double-decker at the age of five,
Lying between the wheels
The smell of petrol
The horror on the face of the driver
My embarrassment

From then I change
Doubted my parents' authenticity
Woke up in the middle of a football game
Bodies dragging against one another
Someone offers a pill
Lay down on the street when a car came
Two girls and me in a tarpaulined vehicle
Showing our sex

The penny-bare-bums
Slot machine arcades
Saturday morning flicks
Eyes burnt-out
Body staked down for ants and vultures,
Attached to a tree
Like a pin-cushion with arrows,
Naked limbs in a warm wet hollow
Between leaves,
Since then defiled

Snow storm in a bubble
That falls eternally

Woke up again
Driving a van onto a slip-way

I died as a child

# A ROUGH GUIDE TO AVIGNON

Sylvester the Second, pope in Occitan,
One time student in the schools of Toledo

Where Muslim scholars delved in alchemy,
Had a bronze head which warned his holiness

Of all impending danger.  Even today his tomb
Rattles and sweats before a pontiff dies

Clement the Fifth decamped from Italy
With a motley crew of harlots, gluttons, cheats,

Settled eventually in Avignon, but died
Of a plate of ground up emeralds
Prescribed for indigestion

John the Twelfth acquired a magic knife,
With which he enchanted the conclave of cardinals

And so ensured succession. His friend, King Phillip
Gave him an amulet of serpents' tongues

Encrusted with wondrous gems
That changed their colour
On contact with poison

Benedict found the treasure of the Jews
Sealed it up in a room in the form of golden statues

And still those statues stand unseen, though once
Three women came from Venice to remove
A flagstone, leading to that secret chamber,
And found

Only a bottomless abyss

## THE PLANETS

Drifting across a blue planet

Wings on your heels as fast as hummingbirds,
Apparently motionless,
You look down on hazy islands,
Worlds of sand, impenetrable forests,
Cities of stone on dizzy pinnacles,
Tiny vessels lost in immensity,
Little gods who treat you as a brother,
Enwrapped in vines

Drifting across a grey planet

Cities burning, smoke replaces cloud,
Movement of men on plains,
Carts full of babies,
Weighed down by gold and silver,
Wise men on parchment,
Indicating limits

Hovering above a dark planet

Engines turning - pistons – metal running
With sacramental oil, steam rising,
Men with beards
Pointing to diagrams

Skimming across a green planet

Gardens in the sky, and something much like water,
Your image endlessly mirrored
To a billion managed mindscapes,

On your way to meet a few
Untrammelled minds

# A SIGNIFICANT MOON

The moon is almost exactly the same size
As the ornate streetlamp on the traffic island,
Round and white,
Opposite the stores.

Happy couples pull happy children
Past Christmas displays,
The light of which encircles them like haloes.

We are approaching Christmas…

Strange concept.

As if Christmas were a place,
Where, when we arrive,
We could linger,
Set up shop,
Build a permanent dwelling
Like the elves and reindeer
In the toy departments.

That *is* where we would live, given the choice,
If we were honest

In those glittering grottos, surrounded by telescopes,
Space guns that fire colour,
Like the penny arcade shows of Aladdin's cave
When we were children

We would make brief sorties, perhaps, to caravans,
In the summer, lit by gas-lamps,
Near to shady hollows fed by streams
In which we'd bathe,
Or to collect prizes for "progress"
Or sing hymns in front of multi-coloured mounds
Of fruit and vegetables
And tins of beans.

Perhaps that's where we go when we die
Through the back of the wardrobe
Through the swimming mirror

To the small, dark room with armchair seats,
Smelling of leather and tobacco smoke.

In front of a blank screen

Which is about to blossom.

# OLD PERSON IN KIT FORM

It doesn't take a lot
A light dusting of grey
A few lines
A minor correction to the upright posture
And there you are
You have it
An old person

Of course, you can add a smell,
A certain forgetfulness,
A general preoccupation with the past,
Disinterest in fashion
A new way of looking at the young

However,
Not all these are requisite

You can build one in the comfort of your home –
Your home which, too, is receding into the past
Its carpet fraying,
The mounted photographs of long dead children,
Now men

But, really, this is all just the outer shell
Of your model
Ideally it needs a source of power,
Perhaps regret
Perhaps wound up by recrimination
So it can trundle round its floor space,
Not quite avoiding objects
Search for bills already paid
Spill coffee... scald itself...

When complete,
It can be packed away neatly
In a box labelled
*Not for further use*

# CLOACAE

You know,
I really did visit the latrines –
The cloacae
Open now to the sun,
With their crumbled blocks of sandstone

Where they sat and conversed with each other –

Where they did their business –

As sparkling water coursed through sluices,
Naiads disported on marble floors,
Coins mounted steadily in earthenware pots
Whole villages died.

Then readjusting their robes,
They would walk out into the sunlit colonnades,
Where, under the watchful eyes
Of a benign Augustus,
Perhaps they stripped again,
Wrestled their oily flab,
Ran small races in the warm sand,
Gave money to a slave for services rendered.

Later they would receive tribute
In a damasked hall,
Heavy tapestries of old killings,
Peacocks,
Adjusted wigs, and face powder –
The smell of mortality
Disguised by rich unguents from the Ind.

Now they're back in cubicles –
Talking to each other through walls again –
Neon-lit,
In the bogs of power,
Hot water on demand from a gasping planet –
Waving fingers at an unseen beam
Making things vanish.

# CHILD

All those teachers, those parents never knew
The wounded god that walked among them.
The strange primeval worlds that coexisted
With their own.
How beautiful, and vulnerable, and sad
Those eyes that saw
Through their own bricks and tarmac.
Those feet that waded through lush forests.
Saw giant waterfalls, exotic creatures,
And endless sky.

How could they care
For the helpless eternal
Burnt by their casual remarks,
Blown through the air by breath,
Buried below miles of solid rock,

By a single glance.

# EMMERDALE

My mother lives on Emmerdale Farm,
Surprising, really,
Since she's always hated animals

She's there with the livestock,
The intrigue
Breathless at the latest homicide
The current alien abduction

Meantime she's spilling Cup a Soup on her 3 piece

She's concerned about the harvest
While the plant on her windowsill
Gives up the ghost
Through lack of watering

Outside
The trees are dripping sunlight
But she can only see the walls
Wobbling on the telly

My mother lives on Emmerdale Farm

Perhaps it's the safest place for her

Each week the State posts her subsistence
Each week she totters to the gaping supermarket

Trundles between ads
For sports cars and holidays

Sends cards and cash
Dutifully to her grandchildren
Who rarely reply

My mother lives in Coronation Street
Answers no questions in quiz games
But roots for all contestants

Is lost forever in Albert Square,
Blind to the men in sharp suits
Lurking behind the scenery

Will sign any policy, reveal any secret,
To the nearest stranger

My mother lives in Coronation Street
But her real habitation
Is the past

**ON BEAUTY →**

## A PROFOUNDLY DISABLED PHYSICIST TRANSCENDS THE BODY

A foolish grin,

Like some toddler on a fair ride,
He rushes upwards

His body rigidly horizontal,
But curiously weightless

Astounded airmen attempt to restrain him,

But his brittle stick
Eludes their fingers.

He is gone.

Through worm-holes

Along cosmic string pieces

His algebraic clothing falling away from him

Computerised chatter becoming silent

In a giant air balloon.

On a still tornado

Like a big brainy baby

Gone over the rainbow.

# SNOWFALL

The snow falls gently through space

The mind supplies a connection
With the strains of Mozart
From a nearby roof garden

Falling calmly, with complete assurance,

From the high cloud ironically solid,
From the sun-strafed heavens toying with majesty

Kisses the security guard leaning and smoking

Spreads lovingly across the picture of a killer

Blesses the proud trees with their shreds of plastic

The humans scuffling in the backs of removal vans

Settles purely on the tarnished walk-ways

And

Disappears

## A WOMAN IN MIND

I've accepted the inevitable –
That the woman I've constructed in my mind
Is never going to sleep with me

She doesn't have an anus,
At least not one that's used for defecation

She's been poisoned by her own waste products

She has no blood to bleed –
Or carry nutrients –
She's all surface –
Shallow if you will

She looks good in makeup, lipstick, and high heels

She thinks I'm great
But does she have a brain?

That's open to conjecture

She *could* bear children, but without stitches

An epidural won't be necessary

Besides, she was young in the forties
And though she carries her age well,
It's bound to catch up with her eventually

No one speaks like that any more

She's called *Imogen* or something of that kind,

You've never met her, nor ever will, I guess

I fashioned her, like papier-mâché,
Out of old newspapers –
Mainly the News of the World

Sometimes, she's French, or even German,
Never American or Australian –
Sorry

She *does* menstruate, I think,
But only when I'm absent

I should replace her with
Something more substantial, I suppose,
But I'm sentimental, and besides,
She makes few, if any, demands upon me

# THE THIRD DIMENSION

The seagull drifts in three dimensions
Across the backdrop of the loch,

From here no sense of winged exertion,
As bound, and unbound as the rocks,

As free as dreamt birds ply their labours,
As effortless as sun on wind,

And every blade and stone is cradled
In light's half-yearned continuum.

The fences travel in their stillness
Outflanked by thought's hegemony,

And parts of hills are individual,
Have no straight-line geometry.

Sun and stillness slowly gather,
Crystallize round browsing sheep,

In virtual valleys where all matter
Is turned to gold in summer's heat.

# THROUGH THE NET

A whole life spent as a congenital idiot

Childhood
Puberty
Middle-age

All the people you meet
Your sexual feelings
Your draining away of power

Wrinkles
Illness

Never been anything else

Will die as such

Short of stature, stumpy build,
Asiatic features, vacant grin,

How did you slip through the net?
Dodge past needles?

Your conversation is limited
Your allure hard to pinpoint

Some people think God loves you
More than anyone

He has a strange way of showing it

## GODDESSES

Thank God I died,
She says,

Can you imagine,
A draught blowing up my dress,
To reveal thick woolly knickers
And cellulite

Blue veins like cracks in an unglazed vase

Thank God I fulfilled my dream
Of immortality
By dying

Or perhaps being killed

All the better for my legacy
Of doomed erotic innocence

All the better
For your fantasies

**SELF PORTRAIT →**

## IT'S BEEN A GOOD YEAR

It's been a good year
So far
Touch wood.

No major catastrophes
Touch wood.

My mum's still alive,
In a manner of speaking.

Getting older, of course.
No more incoherent than she's ever been

In my case,
No recurrence of the skin cancer
As yet
Touch wood

No lasting damage from the recent mugging
Psychologically speaking

The head wound's coming along nicely

Haven't made any friends yet
In life

But I'm on talking terms with the traffic warden

Well
*I* speak to her

Been a good year
On the whole
So far…

# I HATE LIFE

I hate life, don't you?
Poking its nose in everywhere,
Under every stone,
In every cranny

Comes to visit you on Boxing Day,
To share the turkey,
In the guise of relatives
Or microbes

I hate its persistence -
It won't be denied;
As a squirrel,
It pockets your last plum;
As a tax-collector
It steals your last fiver

It moves in next door to you
With a dark skin
And smells of curry

Or rattles your letterbox
With a National Front brochure

It swarms in your picnic hamper
It scuffles behind your wall

Swims through the rubber membrane,
Teems in its cellular bridgehead

Gasps in the day-centre
Gurgles in intensive-care

Always there when you don't want it.

When you want it,
Never there…

# TWENTY FOUR HOUR DREAMING

I can't remember the last time
I had a proper dream

You know,
One where you're slashing muggers
Across the neck
With metal,

Watching yourself appearing on stage
In a huge theatre,

Sitting at a lone table
Turning on a lamp,
Shivering,

Being visited by people from another planet
Whom you recognise
Telling you it's time

My dreams are full of job interviews
That almost go quite well

Journeys on buses that do not explode
To houses steadfastly similar
To when you saw them last

In my dreams I listen to radio broadcasts
Telling of wars, and global warmings –

Eat toast,

And talk for long hours with people
I don't find particularly interesting

# MY FIRST WAGE PACKET

I bought people drinks
But they were the wrong people -

My friend whose love spills over into violence,
Another who passed the drinks on to someone else
And took the credit.

I thought of the great explorers,
Loaded with gunpowder and printing presses
Who travelled roads of silk, crossed terrible bays –
Now traversed in seconds.

On my grave I will have an advert for kebabs
Rent out space to local prostitutes
People will carouse from my plastic cup
Tossing out the flowers.

My grandchildren will feature in snuff movies,
Assuming they survive the casting couch,
Those mute inglorious Miltons delivering leaflets
For double-glazing firms.

*DANGER OF DEATH* will be their epitaph,
Or perhaps *NO DUMPING,*
Or *DICK GAG AND BEN DOVER*
*ALSO LIE HERE.*

A black-bordered invitation to dissect earthworms,
Sweeping away the dinner plates and candelabra,
Post-prandial coition, evening dress,
Brandy and cigars.

Archimedes used his wife apparently
To illustrate displacement of bath water,
Her thrashing limbs at first hindering the experiment
Until she finally succumbed.

## MY MOTHER

My mother watches me
In case I turn on a light,
Follows me about the flat
To head off consumption.

Stands in the kitchen doorway,
In the gathering dark,
Short and defiant,
Watching.

I sit in the armchair,
See the heavy blossom
Over the grass courts,
And wonder, does she ever sit,
And what does *she* see.
What does the birdsong mean to her,
If anything.

She never liked animals - or children.

## VINTAGE POISON

I've begun to speculate on the heights of buildings.
The trajectory of a fall.
The material impacted upon.
Curiously the possibility of passers-by
Doesn't unduly concern me,
Apart from their effect on the final result.

I take more interest in knives
And blunt objects;
Poison, carcinogens, though radiation
Seems still a little rarefied,
If becoming more common.

Death or serious injury as a topic of conversation
Remains somewhat frowned on
In polite society,
But I do slip in the odd reference
To the availability of firearms
In certain parts of London.

Why the interest?
It's hard to pinpoint.
But it may have something to do
With you.

**THE PRESENT →**

## DOG DAYS

The women are craning their necks
To look into dress shops.

They do not see me at all.

I'm craning my neck to look at the women.

An Indian is attempting to give away forests
Outside the tube station.

Peace, in a Roman war-chariot,
Runs amok above the toilets.

Time is running out
For the urban foxes.

These are difficult days…

# REAL ESTATE

I'm looking to buy a house in London, you know –
Anything considered
Not too expensive
Pleasant aspect
Moat
Portcullis
Barbed wire…search-towers…

I've got a sniffer dog already –
Gets a bit irritating.
I've taken him to the vet but...
No… He can sniff out Muslims
At twenty paces –

You've got to be so careful, these days…

Where I'm living now
We've all clubbed together
For our own private police-force,
And executioner

I'm followed everywhere
By my claims solicitor

Got three kids –
They're still in the womb
Safer
Privately-educated, of course
We communicate by ultrasound –
Quality time!

Well, tea-break at the office, actually.
Means I'm still accessible to clients.

Wife gave me a wonderful gift for my 40<sup>th</sup> birthday
24 hour wakefulness!
Hard-wired
Didn't even have to stay in overnight.

Means I'm still accessible to clients .

Life is good…
Well, not really...

But…bearable…
Well, not really…

## TRIBUTE

Worthy of note the processes involved

Thinking backwards, or forwards,

From the wilting flowers,

Tied to a railing

And not impossible
To ascertain the facts

Though you probably never will

Better not to experience
The stock response,
To addict, or prostitute,
Elder, or child,

Just a long succession of absences,
Of empty chairs,
Virtual lovers,
Or victims

Forms no longer relevant

See the solid state universe,
Of this unknown brother,

The four dimensions
Of this

Completed
Line

# THE AVANT-GARDE

*As early as 1913 I had the happy idea*
*to fasten a bicycle wheel to a kitchen stool*
*and watch it turn…*

*A few months later I bought a cheap reproduction*
*of a winter evening landscape*
*which I called "pharmacy",*
*after adding two small dots, one red and one yellow*
*in the horizon.*

Meanwhile, some cunt in England
Put a teacosy on his head
And renamed his country estate
*"Do As Thou Wilt"*

Oh, let me be avant-garde
I.e. only one hundred years behind the times

Let me live in a world of casual sex and hangovers.
May my hair stick up at right angles.

My favourite film be *Cabaret,*
My favourite pose one of pre-Nazi dilettantism.

Let me be convinced I can topple governments
By reciting the Lord's Prayer backwards.

Be pursued across Europe by agents
Who mistake my objets trouvés
For terrorist weapons.

Let me take plaster-casts of my own cock
And live somewhere near Dalston.

# TOO MANY FAT AMERICANS

Too many people.

Too much Art, Literature, Music, Architecture,
Picking over of the "Classics".

Too many soaps, sporting events, entertainments,
Celebrities – alive or dead, high-brow and low.
Too much "freedom" – or not enough.

Too many cross-overs between religions.
Too much access, too much history,
Too much health.
Too much compassion for the starving masses.
Too many charities, mail-shots, lovers, diseases,
Panaceas, fulfilments…

Too many speeches, rebuttals,
Resistance to oppression –
Too many rapes and rose gardens,
Tapes for relaxation.
Too many business lunches, back-street abortions,
Theories of creation, solid-fuel heating systems.
Too many sincere apologies,
Brave but ultimately futile attempts at originality,
Fashion accessories

Too many tits, arses, vaginas,
Buggies, wheelchairs,
Too many dental appointments,
Holiday homes, sewers, rodents,
Reckless romances,
Visionary experiences, depressions…

Too many worthy black men, wise Orientals,
Canny Scots, humourless Germans -
And fat Americans…

Too many cars, too many sustainable resources,
Too much sea, too much sky,
Too many stars, all jockeying for attention,
Too many nebulae,

Too many poets, too many rhymes –
Internal or otherwise –
Too
Many
Words

## RANDY BLOCKS GAVIN'S JAB WITH
## A *WOO DAH*

The Shaolin monks are breaking bricks again,
Great piles of them, across their shaven heads,
Breasts transfixed with medieval darts

They're moving into the Arts Centres,
Soaking up the grants

They've got nice bodies and attract the gays.

They rise from dry ice in a welter of oriental intrigue,
Their heads ribbed and glinting in the arc-lights.

They've taken to make-up and wearing tights,
Swapped kung fu slippers for ballet pumps

The old master watches from the wings,
Enigmatically, a knowing smile
Playing across his lips.

They say he's their agent, takes fifteen per cent
Of everything they make,

But some there are
who say he's paid only in gold,

Which he melts down and pours,
When evening stars and signs are favourable
Into a Buddha mould

# AMONG TORTURED CHICKENS

The light has been drained of all nutrients,

*Special offer on sheep's testicles!*

So much choice!
A snowstorm of shape and colour!
Instant disability as you pass the security camera

The plastic Guantanamo Bay is electronically tagged

The wafer-thin ham has fallen through
The wafer-thin carrier bag

Hate your neighbour as yourself!

Am I my brother's gaoler?

Log jam of trolleys around the rotten fruit

Fighting has broken out over the boxed fungus

The staff have opened fire
Many dead and wounded

Can we blend them?

**TERROR →**

# NIGHT-WATCHMAN

How can you bear those voices,
Hardly distinguishable,
Through the curtains,
On the street below?

Can you put a face to them,
Old or young?

Like the trim figure of a woman
With long hair,
Who turns
And shows a face
Ravaged by time

This girl was a fine girl –
She had arms, and legs,
And all her senses

But I'm a night-watchman –
I watch over the night

See what I've caught
In my untended nets

## THE PROGRAM

Presumably torture is computerized nowadays.

What program do they use?

Do they have Windows for defenestration?

Are photos of victims scanned, and then burned
Using Nero

Are deaths "encrypted"?

But, of course,
Bureaucracy is part of the torturer's craft -
Sleep-deprivation has to be logged...

Eyes gouged out accounted for
In departmental records

Even a practice that officially isn't happening
Has to be monitored as cost-effective

"I"s have to be dotted,
"T"s crossed,
Unmarked graves marked somewhere
When the file's closed.

# A SONNET FOR DR. HAROLD SHIPMAN

Dr. Harold Shipman would have pleased my mum -
He made good use of all his education;

Suave and well-spoken, though offending some
With his tendency to kill. In mitigation,

One could argue that he felt a kind of pity
Among all those moth-balled frocks and dentures – Joe

Orton would have been a shade more witty,
But would have understood. And shall he go

To Hell, now that he too lies on a slab
After slow-strangulation with a sheet

Tied to a bar – an ending no less drab
Than those he gave to patients that he'd treat…

Some wail he cheated justice, some rejoice –
"Let him who's free from sin" would be my choice.

# SINK THE TITANIC!

We're on the Titanic
Forget the film

Stand in the corner and don't think
Of a twelve-foot high rabbit –

The band is playing
The women are getting made up
The children are living their best nightmare

And you
Putative male
Will do what?
Raid the bar?
Settle in to a posh cabin?
Become T.V.?

As the rats come up from below
In staggering numbers,
And the iceberg looms off
To its next appointment…

Read poetry?

## SAME OLD

That person you see every day,
Doing the same thing,
Absurdly tall,
Opening a door for people with money,
Wearing a brown bowler hat,
Selling flowers –

That life, immobile, wearing away
Like a rock in breakers –
Those thoughts trying to contain themselves,
That watch, ruthless, that till
Opening and shutting with finality

Set your clock by him,
Measure the seasons,
See him turn grey, the hair fall,
Watch him fixed in the constellations -

As *he* watches you.

# A SERVICEABLE WAR

We need a war.

A war that can be declared
And nobody notices.

A war without a clear beginning and end

We need a conflict

That doesn't disturb shopping patterns.
One that can be fun,
Have entertainment value,
Be almost fashionable.

We need a war that doesn't discriminate
In terms of race, gender,
Or sexual inclination.
A war which displays heroism
And family values
In a saleable manner.

We need a clean war – even sanitized,
A war to end *all* wars
But which doesn't ever end itself...

We need a war of sufficient magnitude,
That looks good from a distance,
That inspires youth, and awakens memories
In the senior citizens

A war with élan,
A distinguished war,
A war subtly stimulating
In a good way –
A war to die for...

**HAVE YOUR SAY →**

## LOCAL ELECTION RESULTS 2007

What do you think of the new mass-murderer
Who's taken over the corner-shop?

He seems very nice
His wife's really tasty
Three lovely kids
And he's offering
A *two-for-one* deal on cream crackers

Of course, people object
To the smell from his garden,
The stench of burnt flesh

I'm keeping our cat in for the time being -
She came back with a human hand
Soon after they arrived

But he's promised to put in higher walls
And more security cameras
And the lawn is impeccable!

All in all
I think he'll be good for property prices,
And he's promising to take on
Some part-time assistants.

## HAVE YOUR SAY

The policeman can afford to be nice
He has a gun

He tells me if I've nothing to hide,
I've got nothing to fear.

He's just accessed my bank statements.

After all, he says,
If I *was* a terrorist I'd want to be protected
Against myself.

My next door neighbour is very keen on Terror –
That, and paedophiles;
It's a kind of hobby with him.

*He tells me* the milkman has been acting strangely
And to check the tops on all bottles.

He once saw a father
Fondle a child, he says,
And looked up his sex-rating on the internet –

The man was clean, it's true, but even Hitler
Had to start somewhere –

When the Muslims were interned,
He suggested a national holiday
On the People's Parliament website,
And got a commendation
From the UK President.

## CHANGING GUARD AT BUCKINGHAM PALACE

Always this need to make things more than human...
Kings and princes, soldiers in tall hats –
Two minutes silence for immortal deaths...

I'm excited by a coach, then realise
It must do the rounds for the tourists...

Sirens wail, vans rush past each other,
Lights flashing.

Something is happening here,

The end of something. A beginning.
Even the sun is silent for two minutes –
But without compassion.

Tears in the eyes of someone in a wheelchair,
Victoria borne aloft, mounted policemen,

A roundabout that's stopped revolving,
Figures in their summer frocks

Turned permanently to stone.

## OUTRAGE

God does not distinguish.

He has no favourite sons or daughters.

He doesn't get sentimental about the charlady
Who was blown up in Tavistock Square,
And is indifferent to whether
She was likeable or not.

There *are* no chosen people –
They simply choose themselves.
And there are no outcasts –
They cast themselves out,
Or try to.

The death of fifty-one people in a terrorist outrage
In Central London has no less pathos
Than the death of one forgotten pensioner
Rotting undiscovered in a council flat,
But no more

And the next time they ask you
To observe two minute's silence,
You should tell them
You have been silent for too long,
You have observed a most profound silence
Since the day you were born,
Since your conception

The only real evil is unreality,
The stock-in-trade of politicians and advertisers,
And the least exalted spectacle
Is that of people trying to make money
Or gain power, which is much the same thing,
From blood-stained body parts.

Fly from the man
Who makes you feel good about yourself,
Tells you that you are brave,
Put-upon,
Long-suffering.

You *deserve* nothing.
You *have* no rights,
Except those you are willing to resign
For the benefit of others.

Any blame can only be safely attached to yourself.

Why did you do it?

# THE NAMER OF NAMES

There is someone, somewhere, or a group of people
Whose job it is to give *names* to things.

To make unpalatable truths palatable,
Or to undermine others by nomenclature, or *naming*

*Insurgents* do not *surge in* from outside
To cause disruption…

The word *terrorist* describes
A method, not a system of ideas…

A *holocaust* is something that's burnt whole,
Not a defining point in history…

A zone where nothing flies…

A word which makes clear thought impossible…

Eyes that are scanned for irregularity…

Minds that are tagged on to a database…

The print of a voice betrays non-Aryan roots…

The science of skulls made perfect on the screen

# THE LITERARY
# SCENE →

# A STRANGE EXPERIENCE

Wayne tells me of a strange experience

Something to do with an old flame
And a public toilet

Two blokes whacking one off
To the strains of Vivaldi
In separate cubicles,
The "Four Seasons", he thinks

Wayne has low self-esteem,
Despite being a published poet

After a few drinks he has a tendency
To attack women, or at least fantasize
About smashing in their faces

But only strangers

And ones with whom
He senses a rapport

Sometimes I think it's fortunate
He lives in Chelmsford

And generally leaves early
To catch his night bus

## MY AGENT

My agent tells me my best hope
Of breaking in to the literary scene

Is to commit suicide
In a public manner

It seems like sound advice –
He's never let me down before.

In more detail,
He recommends I leave
Sundry poems
Short stories
And treatments for screen plays
Scattered around my body
With a suicide note,
Tasteful, and gently self-deprecating,
Dedicated to Andrew Motion.

He assures me he will capitalize
On the resulting publicity
To broker a deal with a top publishing house

I'm considering it

## VERSE IS EASY

I was thinking about the vicissitudes
Of human experience

Of the man who ate a Chinese meal
And the next day his arms and legs fell off

Of hard-working villagers surprised
By the Asian Tsunami

Of how, once,
Halfway through a deathless sonnet
My biro ran out

Have you noticed how the depression
That follows a night of failure
Is subtly different
From that after a night of success?

A poet once told me that verse is easy,
Just a question of flushing the poem out
From its hiding-place, or like a sculptor
Removing the excess from a block of marble
To reveal the pre-existing masterpiece

Unfortunately, as a writer, he was shit

I'd like to take up dry stone walling, really,
But nowadays it's all done with computers

Also, I once saw a false leg
Propped up against a goldfish tank
But failed to derive inspiration from it

# STRINDBERG

He dwelt in a red room, clambered over tables,
Upsetting the absinthe

Kissed for a full sixty seconds,
Admired by luminaries of the Nineteenth Century.

Was married to several fictional characters,
Including a goddess.

Visited Hell on a regular basis.

Was punished by trolls of a mythical potency.

Followed throughout by the stench of humanity

Fearful of dogs, ravens, and flutterings in the keyhole

Longed for a modest garden near the sea,
A faithful wife and children,

Instead, got hangovers and immortality

## BEST PRACTICE

He doesn't do it right

He drinks and smokes until
His face becomes like putty
Makes a nuisance of himself
With the emergency services

Rails against people with cars and children

Visits his doctor and complains
Of his own longevity

He writes verse like a rat trying
To escape from a kitchen

Holds a pen
As one would hold a knife
In the presence
Of a faithless loved one

He should stay in bed longer

Not thrust his face into the faces
Of real people,
But those in dreams

All his concern should be
For imaginary bills

That's the proper way to do it

## CHELSEA

Chelsea comes from mixed-race parents
And is somewhat overweight

She fears death in a fire
Started by herself, and often flees
Her flat, half-clothed and barefoot,
Making towards the Palace,
Uncertain why.

She'd like to start a business producing postcards,
But in the meantime,
Takes her medication.

# NARNIA

This is the land where dreams come true
In Narnia

Where cloven-footed gentlemen
Who quote the classics
Accost ya'
Especially if you're children

This is the land of friendly uncles
Dripping bear flesh
Dwarves a drowning
Where *you* too can be queen for fifteen minutes
In Narnia

This is the tree with its branch through Heaven
To Narnia
Where even if you're common
You can talk with demons
In Narnia

Where pointy hats and scimitars
And jewel-encrusted caliphs
Are put to flight by pipe-smoking
Dons in carpet slippers

Where you jump off a precipice
And fall forever

Stifle in your nightmare
On a fog-bedevilled island

Read a book which is *you,*
Screaming in every bookcase

In Narnia

# THE POET LAY ON THE TABLE, DEAD

Number One Thousand in the Penguin Verse,
Baring her soul to all posterity,
Revealing father-hate, despair, and worse,
Clinical depression plain to see;

Her lover lags Nine-Hundred-and-Seventy-Six,
Obsessed with killer fish and rotting sheep,
Nature's brutality a kind of fix –
Too brutal himself, perhaps, to care to weep.

Both of them rotting now, and paper mites
Feeding upon their life's experience,
They posture in borrowed bodies in the light
That's frozen in the colour supplements…

And we, unable to profit by their pain,
Pull down the blinds, and turn the page again.

**THE FUTURE →**

# A BAD START

Heavily-armed Arabs are manning checkpoints
On the Portobello Road.

Straight, white males are forming ghettos.

Pogroms have been forecast.

Genetically-mutated models,
With breasts supported by shopping trolleys,
Clutter the dress shops.

I adjust my spacesuit,
Step out gingerly onto the King's Road;
Nylon football strips balloon past
In the keening wind,
The horizon glowing red

Goths, Trekkies, Neo-Mongols

I'm not sure who owns the district

I finger my blaster.

Buskers perform full penetration as I pass,
On the off-chance…

An immigrant gives birth

Body parts are exchanged furtively
In shop doorways

A middle-class couple point out places of interest
To a fresh-faced boy

"Get down!" I scream, release a volley.

The boy's head disappears.

The parents look confused, perhaps reproachful.

I slip them my insurance details.
As a radioactive foxtail
Flashes behind a dumpster

Bad start.

I take a happy pill.

## PEASANTS PRESENTING HARVEST GIFTS TO HENRY THE LION

I know the nightmare is coming
One way or the other,
From within or from without

In the days of hurricanes and spitting fire,
When our children circle in the heavens,
Battling with eagles, and the mangy dragon,

We'll want to blend, obscure, expunge the images,
Scramble communications,
Negate our statements as soon as they are made,

Losing contact with our soldiers in the field.
Each one will fight on alone,
Falling mostly from friendly-fire.

Our radio signals are attracting comets,
Our dreams invaded by men in suits,
The keeper of the keys has been arrested
While censors screen our eyes.

A hole has appeared in my cranium,
Releasing molten rock and noxious gases,
Bipolar policemen are abducting my grandchildren,
Making ransom demands in the guise of fines

Near-life experiences are becoming common -
I met your god at the supermarket recently,
Panic-buying tins of food and toilet rolls.

I mostly delegate my identity card
To do my business, attend social functions.
It's safer to stay at home
Watching old encounters, and previous lives.
I bought a retirement home on the sun
But they froze my pension;

I could downsize I suppose -
It's cheaper to live there -
But what's the point of going anywhere:
*I* always insist on coming too…

# THE OUTER-RING ROAD

The emergency services criss-cross the city –
A death here
A life there
The 22's stack up.

Various winged and pedal-driven vehicles
Attempt to save the planet.
Men search for new body-parts to pierce.
Women disappear behind tattoos
Of glamorous celebrities.

The new millennium is receding –
Eschatological utopian fantasies
Are proving unreliable.

The sun, unaccountably,
Proceeds as normal

Models sport the latest tags,
Pout at cameras.
The old trundle to day-centres
In iron lungs –
They are probably immortal.

I moved my furniture into my saloon car
Becalmed on the outer-ring road
Since 2007.
I've put my name down for two gay sons
And a saleable daughter.
The traffic cop is immobile,
Mummy bandages flapping in the purple wind –

If you are reading this, then all is well –
If not…

**ON THE SOUL →**

## NOT STOPPING BY WOODS ON A
## SNOWY EVENING

What is it that makes up for the day?

The loss of it?

Time and space experienced
Through an open window
With the radio on

Strange facts, and consumer tips;
Some dishes left
With water and detergent sliding away

What birds are felt
Pecking on the newly-hoovered carpet,

What slips of paper
Shiver on a board to remind us
Of leaves

And when we wait,

What message down the line will spread its wings,
Carry us with it
Beyond lumps near hedgerows

With their faint, rancid smell of recognition

What sun will run through tubes
To convince us
That, really, we are light.

# THOUGHTS OF A FRIEND

On an intercity bus

Jeremy Wilson says we're all asleep

He says he knows it

When the light falls across faces,
Flickering on and off
From speeding cars

And a body passes, perched on two wheels,
Teasing death

It may have something to do with the monotonous
Hum of the engine, he tells me, or the rolling road,
The enforced idleness

But it's then he knows

The faces that attract him, and those that don't

Those with eyes closed, or stolidly awake

Those that look innocent – and those grotesque,
With sagging jaws

Even his own face which he almost sees,

Reflected in the dark glass of the window pane,

Are all

Asleep

# THE UNFURNISHED ROOM

Locke said the mind is an unfurnished room.

Bare boards lightly stained
With a thin layer of dust,
Not stirring in the shaft of sunlight,
Through the uncurtained window

Painted plaster peeling with infinitesimal slowness,
Sunlight never waning in the long afternoon

And the sense of something huge, like a garden,
Or an empty street, as in childhood,
Domestic, familiar, not colonnades,
Through the filmy pane

Track the boards for discarded items -
An empty cotton-reel, a broken toy,
To give some clue of time or place,
Or a box whose lifted lid
Would reveal the searched-for secret

Pearl necklace, cameo brooch, or medal,
Cigarette cards, or soldier's buttons

Wander then, feet just above the floor,
In the vast silence, to the panelled door

The handle brass reflecting dully
Your looming shape as you approach the key

Then stop. Your dreaming body frozen there

At the sound of something
Moving
On the stair

# HERE BE HUMANS

This is the woman.
This is how she gets up in the morning.
This is how she spends her day.
This is her bag, full of lipstick
Red as blood.

These are the men.
Who stand in proud rows, presenting arms.
All shapes and colours –
They wear different helmets and headdresses,
But their bodies are unclothed.

These are the children.
They are neither men nor women.
They are process.

This is an old person.
A wrinkled shell that once was human.
It too is neither male nor female.

It is residue.

I peel back the skin to reveal

Eternity

# THE RUNNER OF LITTLE RACES

Cut up into manageable segments
His life became unmanageable.

He took to heart the parable of the hare
And tortoise, and emulated the time-keeper,
Changing his name to *Zeno* in the process.

A simple table leg, he reasoned,
In his untidy kitchen
Might contain untold worlds,
Each with their own philosophies.
He took to rescuing furniture from skips
And stacking it in his bedroom.

A single piece of hamburger
Might be ultimately indivisible –
This led him to become vegetarian.

Eventually he built a computer
The size of the known
And unknown
Universe,
And arriving at an action
Irreducible in its selflessness,
He labeled it "God"…

But was uncertain
How to proceed further…

# THE GARDEN

Some, when they were planted,
Grew up as stones,
And some as trees

Some came back as roses

Some flowered on Sundays in pinks and greens

Some mouldered unearthed as cuddly toys,
Mainly the young ones

Some proclaimed as angels, only to crack
And fall with splintered wings and broken backs

Some, no more bold than when they were alive,
Scarcely disturbed the surface

Some preferred
A second or so of glory,
Streaming in sunlit smoke above the stack
And vanished then forever,
Ingested by relatives and passers-by.

Some parsimonious,
Grew up in plastic petals, coloured tape

Some formed the symmetry of a funeral wreath

Some were raised joyously and knew a peace
In Adam's bosom, safe from dust

Some were uncertain and constrained to trust

Some grew garrulous,
Discovered hidden talents as authors,
Wrapped their words
In plastic sheeting to withstand the rain

Some simply sank into the earth,
Declining ever to return again